Religious Experience

Philosophy of Religion Study Guide

Matthew Livermore

First published 2014

by PushMe Press

Mid Somerset House, Southover, Wells, Somerset BA5 1UH

www.pushmepress.com

© 2014 Inducit Learning Ltd

British Library Cataloguing in Publication Data
A catalogue record for this book is available from the British Library

ISBN: 978-1-909618-44-2 (pbk)
ISBN: 978-1-909618-45-9 (ebk)
ISBN: 978-1-910252-96-3 (hbk)
ISBN: 978-1-910252-97-0 (pdf)

Typeset in Frutiger by booksellerate.com
Printed by Lightning Source

A rich and engaging community assisted by the best teachers in Philosophy

philosophy.pushmepress.com

Students and teachers explore Philosophy of Religion through handouts, film clips, presentations, case studies, extracts, games and academic articles.

Pitched just right, and so much more than a textbook, here is a place to engage with critical reflection whatever your level. Marked student essays are also posted.

Contents

Introduction

KEY WORDS

- **A POSTERIORI** - Applied to reasoning from experience, from effect to cause.

- **ANALOGY** - A correspondence in certain respect between things otherwise different.

- **COGNITIVE** - Capable of truth or falsity.

- **EPISTEMOLOGICAL** - Relating to knowledge.

- **FALLACY** - An apparently genuine but really illogical argument.

- **INDUCTION** - Reasoning from particular cases to general conclusions.

- **MATERIALIST** - One who holds the theory that there is only one substance, namely matter.

- **PEAK EXPERIENCE** - An experience infrequent and emotionally charged. (Maslow)

- **PHYSIOLOGICAL** - Relating to the body.

- **REDUCTIVE (OF A THEORY)** - Narrowing, limiting or making simpler in order to understand.

- **THOUGHT EXPERIMENT** - Hypothetical situation used by philosophers to demonstrate argument.

- **VERIDICAL** - Coinciding with fact; an experience that corresponds to a true state of affairs.

WHAT IS RELIGIOUS EXPERIENCE?

Religious Experience can be one of the more accessible topics when studying Philosophy of Religion. After all, everyone has experiences, and some of them can be unusual, even inexplicable - so there is, for many students, a connection with their own life that is absent from say, Religious Language. However, this topic is also a wide-ranging one, bringing in an immense variety of different types of experience, and many different theories. The sheer variety is one reason why you will find so many different attempts to categorise and break down religious experiences into types. In this chapter I will give an overview of these attempts.

It may surprise you to learn that, according to research by Alister Hardy and David Hay, 30-50% of the British public have reported an experience of a presence or power different from their everyday self. Of these experiences many interpreted them religiously, but a significant number did not give them a specifically religious interpretation. This raises some interesting questions. Is religious experience more common than people usually believe? Could it be under-reported because of fear of ridicule? And if people are reporting experiences without interpreting them religiously, does this undermine the sceptic's claim that religious people "manufacture" religious experiences, perhaps unconsciously, out of the beliefs they have been brought up with?

With this research we come up against some of the trickier problems surrounding religious experience. And we should also be able to see straight away one of the key issues surrounding **A POSTERIORI** arguments - the same experience may be viewed by two people quite differently. But before we examine some of the philosophical implications, we should tackle the question of how to define religious experience.

We are immediately thrown into the heart of the problem if we try and begin with a definition of the term. As **ROBERT SHARF** puts it: "The problem with the term 'experience', particularly with respect to its use in the study of religion, is that it resists definition by design ... the term is often used rhetorically to thwart the authority of the 'objective' or the 'empirical', and to valorise instead the subjective, the personal, the private."

This has been recognised among philosophers for a long time. **THOMAS HOBBES** (1588-1679) said: "What is the difference between saying "God appeared to me in a dream" and "I dreamt I saw God"?" The problem is an **EPISTEMOLOGICAL** one, and attempts to solve it often rely on more fundamental assumptions about the ways in which we can know. We will examine questions related to this later in the book.

There are some generally agreed ways of going about analysing religious experience. One starting point is to look at the actual variety of types of experience that religious people have had. For instance, William James found experiences such as visions, voices, conversion experiences, and group, or corporate, experiences.

When analysed this way we can see something distinctive - religious experiences appear to be analogous with sensory experiences. **CAROLINE FRANKS DAVIS** has described them as "... something akin to a sensory experience"; "... an intellectual intuition which is analogous to our intuition of other human persons in so far as firstly, it is mediated by signs and secondly, it terminates in spiritual reality"; and "... a roughly datable mental event which the subject is to some extent aware of".

Our knowledge of other humans, which is mediated through our senses, is presented here as an analogy for our knowledge of God. In this case we might expect that the senses we use to experience God would be like sight, hearing, and so on, but somehow different. And of course a large part of religious experience is claimed to be visions and voices. But there are two problems with this. First, of course, with seeing and hearing, if we have any doubts about the truth of our perception we can check other people's perceptions of the same object. This is obviously more difficult with religious experience. The second problem is that all kinds of different experiences are claimed to be religious, such that many categories have been created for them.

One of the reasons such a profusion of different categories has arisen in this area is that different religions have different ultimate concerns. Monotheism has focused on the idea of a relationship with a personal loving creator, whereas Eastern religions may have an impersonal identification of self with the supreme reality (as in Brahman in Hinduism), or even an experience of the illusory nature of all existence (as in the Buddhist concept of "nibbana").

Because of these differences, some have sought to redefine religious experience. The psychologist **ABRAHAM MASLOW** coined the term **PEAK EXPERIENCE** to describe euphoric or blissful states, whether in a religious context or not. This was an attempt to naturalise them, and perhaps to show that religious experiences exist in a continuum with lots of other experiences - aesthetic, sensual and so on. It could be that a focus on what makes religious experience unique has ignored the qualities it shares with other experience. For instance, there would be many who would be willing to testify to the experience of calm, balance and wellbeing that come with dancing. These feelings have a clearly **PHYSIOLOGICAL** basis. Why would we separate religious experience out from this and say that it alone has a supernatural origin? Especially when particular practices associated with religions seem designed to have certain physiological effects, for instance prayer, chanting,

5

meditation, ritualised actions and repetitive movements, which often seem to give rise to mind-states which could be characterised as euphoric, calm, blissful and so on.

The problem with this approach is that it confuses feelings with experiences. The Stanford Encyclopedia of Philosophy puts it this way:

> If a subject feels a general feeling of happiness, not on account of anything in particular, and later comes to believe the feeling was caused by the presence of a particular person, that fact does not transform the feeling of happiness into a perception of the person.

In other words, a religious experience must be an experience of a religiously significant reality, and not just a feeling of calm or bliss. However, the interpretation could be seen to be all-important here. For instance, a feeling of relief may come about after an unpleasant trip to the dentist, and no one would call it a religious experience. But if, after long prayer and reflection on my past sins during an Easter vigil service, a feeling of relief and lifting of burdens came over me, I might be far more tempted to call this a religious experience, even if no "being" revealed themselves.

The question of whether a feeling can count as an experience is an interesting one. James, with his interest in mystical experience, proposed feeling as the basis of religious experience, and **RUDOLF OTTO** (1869-1937), who we will look at in a later chapter, also accounts for religious feelings in this way. Both of these thinkers have been influenced to some extent by **F D E SCHLEIERMACHER** (1768-1834), who characterised religious experience as "creature-feeling", and a "feeling of absolute dependence".

So the first issue that arises when considering religious experience is that valid physiological, psychological and sociological explanations exist which seem to make any supernatural explanation superfluous. We will return to this in later chapters.

However, it is worth looking briefly at some of the more recent studies into this fascinating area where brain physiology meets experience. The studies by **MICHAEL PERSINGER** using electromagnetic stimulation of the brain to induce feelings of a "presence", or the Good Friday Experiment by **WALTER PAHNKE** in which the psychoactive drug psilocybin was taken in the context of a church service, are both interesting examples of the area where religion meets neuroscience. The recent studies involving observation of brain scans in meditating Buddhist monks and Franciscan nuns are also fascinating, prompting questions about the nature of consciousness and free will.

The problem that James saw in physiological or psychological explanations of religious experience is not just that they are **REDUCTIVE**, because reduction is often a very useful tool to help us understand phenomena. It is that these reductive explanations are often taken as the last word on religious experience. **CS LEWIS** called this "nothing-buttery" - the idea that the soul is nothing but the collection of electro-chemical signals of the brain, or that religious experience is nothing but an expression of a repressed infant trauma. James saw clearly that the psychology of the person having the experience was profoundly important, but he believed it to be a mistake to claim that it was only the psychology that created that experience. He left open the possibility that there was a reality "on the other side" of the psychological. What reasons did he have for doing this? We shall see in the next chapter.

PHILOSOPHICAL TOOLKIT

You can't do much carpentry with your bare hands, and you can't do much thinking with your bare brain. - Bo Dahlbom

The ability to evaluate arguments well is indispensable in Philosophy. Many students come to the topics armed only with a simple preference for certain theories, and a dislike for others. Much evaluation takes the form of "This theory is poor because it is confusing." In Philosophy, though, we need to be given much sharper and more precise tools of evaluation than the blunt ones of "I like it" or "I don"t like it". Once you realise that not only is there a whole set of tools for assessment of arguments, but that philosophical arguments can also be broken down into more fundamental building blocks which are readily recognisable when you are familiar with them, you will begin to feel more confident, and your assessment and evaluation of arguments will become more sophisticated.

My aim is to give you a philosophical toolkit that you can rely on in an examination, regardless of what question comes up. If you already know some basic philosophical concepts and methods, you will be at a great advantage when it comes to answering, because you will be able to do critical assessment in order to directly answer the question - something which examiners are looking for in the higher-grade answers. List-like or pre-prepared answers which don't quite fit the question are the staple of the student who is stuck in the mindset of memorising knowledge. These kinds of answers are mentioned every year in the examiners' reports as lacking evidence that the candidate can do their own analysis. I can guarantee that by the time you have read this coursebook you will never need to answer in this way.

Induction

Many of the arguments used in this topic will make use of **INDUCTION**. This is because of the nature of religious experience. Inductive arguments are ones that aim to show the probability of something being the case. They usually use generalisations based on observations. For instance, William James researched a large number of testimonies of religious experiences and inductively inferred certain conclusions based on a set of similar characteristics that occurred frequently in them. One of these conclusions was that if one could see a "common core" to very diverse testimonies of religious experience from different traditions, then it was probable that there was a reality which these experiences were giving access to.

Inductive arguments rely on the strength of the observations. Clearly, one of the issues with religious experience is that the observations made are secondhand testimonies, and perhaps more importantly, testimonies of things which are not observable by everyone. For this reason many argue that, given this lack of external confirmation, people who believe they have had a religious experience are simply mistaken.

A posteriori arguments

Any claim based on experience will be a posteriori. Think of the design argument - it uses experience of things such as complexity and regularity in the universe to infer the existence of a God. The key problem with the design argument is that interpretations of the evidence differ. And some interpretations of the complexity of things in the world, such as Darwinism, seem to offer better explanations. Equally with religious experience, all you have to do is show that there is a more plausible alternative explanation than "God did it" for the probability of it being **VERIDICAL** to decrease.

Testimony is one example of a posteriori evidence for religious experience. Hume famously discredited reports of miracles and religious experiences, claiming that they were not reliable. However, Swinburne's principles of credulity and testimony argue against this. These force the burden of proof on to those who say religious experiences are delusions to show why this is the case.

Analogy

The very basis of the idea of religious experience is analogical. For instance, the claim that mystical experience involves a kind of seeing or touching is an **ANALOGY** with sense experience. As **WILLIAM WAINWRIGHT** says, it is on the basis of this analogy that **COGNITIVE** value is ascribed to mystical experience:

> Part of what is implied in ascribing cognitive value to mystical experiences is that these experiences are, in some important respects, like ordinary perceptual experience.

Clearly, the implication with this is that there is something real that is seen or touched in religious experience, and thus that religious experience is veridical.

Remember, analogies work on the basis of likeness. It is not necessary for there to be an exact match between the two things being compared, or clearly there would be no need for analogy!

How good an analogy is is often hard to work out. One way of evaluating analogies is to show where they are like the phenomenon being studied, and where they differ. For instance, **CD BROAD** compares religious experience with musical experience, and says that being tone-deaf, being able to carry a tune, being able to understand music and being a great composer are analogous to a scale of people, ranging from those who have never had any sense of God, to those saints and mystics who have founded religions. He says that the two are similar in some sense because we can trace psychological or genetic factors in both cases which lead to experiences, but the difference is that no one considers musical experience to exist as a reality in itself, so the question of veridicality remains. Of course, this is the very thing that is in question, so some might dismiss this analogy.

Tools for analysis

▸ Correlation is not causation

Just because a link can be established between "types" of highly strung disposition and religious experiences, doesn't mean that the highly strung character is the cause of the religious experience. This is closely linked to the genetic **FALLACY** (see below).

▸ Genetic fallacy

The genetic fallacy is made when an appeal is made to the origin of something which is then used to dismiss it, for instance, if someone said that my belief in God is wrong because my parents gave it to me. But it is hard to decide when to use it, as not all appeals to origins are irrelevant. For instance, Freud's claim that religious experience comes from repressed childhood trauma, if it could be shown to be true, would surely have a bearing on whether it is actually experience of God or a delusion.

▸ The fallacy of the affirmation of the consequent

This is best explained using an example:

- John gets grumpy when he stays up late watching TV.

- John is grumpy.

- Therefore John stayed up late watching TV.

The reason this is a fallacy is that there may be other causes for John's grumpiness, and this is equally applicable to religious experience.

- Normal "perceptual" experiences have a cause beyond the senses in a reality "outside" the perceiver.

- Religious experiences are "perceptual" experiences in some way.

- Therefore religious experiences have a cause beyond the senses in a reality outside the perceiver.

There are clearly all sorts of problems with the above argument. The first is that there are many cases of "perceptions" of things that have no external reality outside the perceiver, for instance, auditory and visual hallucinations; all sorts of pains and feelings. And it is these other interior explanations of "perceptions" which could explain religious "perceptions". But even if we disregard this, there is still a question about the validity of the analogy of perception when applied to a supposedly invisible, intangible being.

▸ Circular arguments

These occur when you assume the existence of the thing you are trying to prove - for example, "God gave us the truths of the Bible. The Bible says God exists. Therefore God exists." Sometimes arguments will undermine themselves because of a similar principle.

▸ Begging the question

This is often levelled at reductive arguments against religious experience. For instance it is easy enough to dismiss religious experience as mere hallucination, but this is really to beg the question, as these experiences are often overwhelmingly felt to be experiences of reality, and so the very question of whether or not they are veridical cannot be assumed to be answered by reference to what a **MATERIALIST** assumes is possible or not possible. According to the mystic, she has just had first-hand experience of why the materialist's worldview is false.

▸ Intuition pumps

This is Daniel Dennett's term for a use of analogy whereby it appears that an argument is being advanced, but in reality there is really only an expression of what one intuitively believes to be the case. He famously used it about John Searle's Chinese Room **THOUGHT EXPERIMENT**. It is important to know that, used carefully, intuition pumps can be useful tools for thinking, as long as they are seen clearly for what they are.

SELF-ASSESSMENT QUESTIONS

1. Research Persinger's Helmet. Does it tell us anything about religious experience? Why, or why not?

2. Find one example of the use of analogy in the topic of religious experience. In what ways are the strengths and weaknesses of analogy evident?

3. Find one example of a circular argument.

4. Find one example of fallacy of affirmation of the consequent.

5. Find one example of the genetic fallacy.

6. Do an informal survey of your friends and family using the question of David Hay: ("Have you ever experienced a presence or power different from the everyday?") If there were answers in the positive, what interpretation does the person give as to why it happened?

7. What is your interpretation?

8. To what extent is it possible to say that a religious experience which occurs under the influence of a psychoactive drug is without merit and non-veridical?

9. What reasons would a reductive materialist give for rejecting an argument from religious experience?

10. Compare peak experiences with other ways of classifying religious experiences. What are the strengths, if any, of classifying them in this way?

FURTHER READING

BAGGINI, J & FOSL, P - The Philosopher's Toolkit, 2nd ed. Wiley Blackwell, 2010

HICK, J - The New Frontier of Religion and Science, Palgrave Macmillan, 2006

WILKINSON, M & CAMPBELL, H - Philosophy of Religion for A2 Level, Continuum, 2009 (Chapter 6)

Aims and main conclusions in The Varieties of Religious Experience

KEY WORDS

- **COMMON CORE** - Belief that there is one divine reality which is common to all religions and is discoverable in religious experience.

- **CONVERSION** - Experience in which someone turns to belief in a divine reality.

- **CRITICAL REALISM** - In epistemology, a theory holding that sense data can tell us about the world, but that we cannot assume that the picture given by that data is fully representative of reality.

- **EMPIRICIST** - Someone who accepts only knowledge based on direct experience.

- **ENLIGHTENMENT** - The spirit of the French philosophers of the 18th C; belief in reason and human progress, and questioning of tradition and authority.

- **INEFFABLE** - Incapable of being described adequately.

- **MYSTICAL EXPERIENCE** - Direct experience of a divine reality.

- **MYSTICISM** - System of mystical thought and experience.

- **NOETIC** - Relating to knowledge (usually non-factual, intuitive).

- **PASSIVE** - A religious experience that the experiencer is unable to exercise control over.

- **PHENOMENOLOGICAL** - Relating to to a philosophical theory which is concerned with describing personal experience without seeking to arrive at metaphysical explanations of them. (Edmund Husserl)

- **PRAGMATISM** - Philosophical methods which makes practical usefulness the test of truth.

- **REDUCTIVE MATERIALIST** - Someone who holds that there can be nothing else than matter. (See also **MATERIALIST**)

- **TRANSIENT** - Fleeting, limited in time.

William James' influential book The Varieties of Religious Experience: A Study in Human Nature, published in 1902, made him an authoritative voice in the study of religious experience. The book focused on **CONVERSION**, saintliness, and **MYSTICAL EXPERIENCE** as it relates to psychology and philosophy.

PRAGMATISM

There are certain important things to realise about James. His training in medicine and psychology led him to emphasise the physiological basis of religious experience - but this did not make him a **REDUCTIVE MATERIALIST**. He was in fact a **PRAGMATIST**. This is evident throughout the Varieties, in phrases such as "God is real since he produces real effects." What this means is that James finds a justification of religion in the subjective utility of religious feelings for the believer. When these feelings are brought into contact with some kind of philosophy or creed - James uses the word hypothesis - about the universe, then there is produced in the believer a state of peace and confidence with long-lasting results.

In the first lecture James makes clear how important this pragmatism is for his project. "Not its origin, but the way in which it works on the whole, is Dr. Maudsley's final test of a belief. This is our own **EMPIRICIST** criterion." He comes to this conclusion after examining and dismissing attempts to explain religious belief in terms of origin:

> In the natural sciences and industrial arts it never occurs to anyone to try to refute opinions by showing up their author's neurotic constitution. Opinions here are invariably tested by logic and by experiment, no matter what may be their author's neurological type. It should be no otherwise with religious opinions. Their value can only be ascertained by spiritual judgements directly passed upon them. Immediate luminousness, in short, philosophical reasonableness, and moral helpfulness are the only available criteria.

We have here clear statements of intent from James as to the nature of his methodology and his aims in examining the testimonies of believers. The three criteria he gives are pragmatic to the core: does the experience shed light on a situation, is it philosophically reasonable, and does it result in improved moral outlook?

It is worth noting that these criteria have a long tradition of use within many established religions as methods of verifying religious experiences, so James wasn't really proposing anything new here. For instance, in Christianity, the words of Christ "By their fruits you shall know them" refers to this nature of judgement. The words of St Paul also echo the same criteria:

> Knowledge puffs up, but charity builds up. If anyone imagines that he knows something, he does not yet know as he ought to know. (1 Cor 8:23)

We have in this short passage the ideas of noetic quality, ineffability and the pragmatic approach to religious experience.

John Hick also proposes this as one of the key tests for validity of religious experience. See also this from James:

> No appearances whatever are infallible proofs of grace. The good dispositions that a vision, a voice, or other apparently heavenly favor leave behind them are the only marks by which we may be sure that they are not possible deceptions of the tempter. (Lecture 1 pp41-2)

Pragmatism seems to be a useful tool when looking at religious experience. **KEITH WARD** interprets James as saying it is sometimes acceptable to believe given insufficient evidence - he says there must be three conditions:

1. It must be a forced option with no alternatives, eg you either have to swim or go down with the ship.

2. It must be vital. It must make a difference to the whole of life.

3. It should be a living choice, not just theoretical; one which comes as a challenge in your culture. This is the thesis presented in The Will to Believe.

Religion is about having a fuller, more vital life, and in that case you can't wait for the evidence. This is key to the Varieties, and it will help us to understand the conclusions James comes to.

RELIGION AS FEELING

James defined religion as "the feelings, act, and experiences of individual men in their solitude, so far as they apprehend themselves to stand in relation to whatever they may consider the divine". It can be seen from this that James is principally concerned with what we might call the experiential rather than the institutional aspect of religion. In fact, James considered the institutional - the communal, doctrinal, public and outwardly ritual forms of religion - to be clearly secondary to the personal, experiential aspect. The institutional was for him an accretion, or later addition to the more primary and essential personal aspect. The primacy of feelings was for James important - these could not be intellectually manufactured and deliberated over - and they pointed to the immediacy of the individual's contact with the divine.

His study was a **PHENOMENOLOGICAL** one, an approach evident from the title of the work. Phenomenologists in the field of religion, such as **MIRCEA ELIADE**, would study the historical and philosophical origins of religious meanings and symbols, whereas James wanted to study the foundations of these symbols in consciousness itself. The approach was a fresh and important one, and it yielded rich results. I will give a brief overview of his main findings.

As mentioned previously, James is influenced by Schleiermacher in certain important respects. This can be seen in the way that he prioritises the feeling of dependence that humans have towards the "primal reality" of the divine. In his conclusion he discerns among all the variety of manifestations a common thread of feeling and conduct which he sets over and against the intellectual formulations and creeds which vary widely between different faiths. In making this **COMMON CORE** argument he proposes the familiar four characteristics of **NOETIC QUALITY, INEFFABILITY, PASSIVITY** and **TRANSIENCY** for mystical experiences, noting that **MYSTICISM** "resembles the knowledge given to us in sensations more than that given by conceptual thought".

Even in this brief overview we can see how central feeling is to his theory, but we will have to make a small detour in order to unpack this tricky concept, and find out the senses in which it has been used, before we can begin to evaluate his aims and conclusions.

In delineating James' aims, methodology and conclusions, it is important to understand the way in which the notion of feeling has come to have such a changed meaning in relation to religious experience since medieval times, when in fact feelings were understood as leading away from, rather than towards, the realm of spirit.

At the time of the **ENLIGHTENMENT** with the philosophy of **IMMANUEL KANT** (1724-1804), a vast change in our understanding of reality and experience took place. A short summary of the key problem posed by Kant is given by the Stanford Encyclopedia of Philosophy:

> *Kant suggests that to take ourselves to have unmediated intellectual access to objects (to have "non-sensible" knowledge) correlates with the assumption that there are non-sensible objects that we can know. To assume this, however, is to conflate "phenomena" (or appearances) with "noumena" (or things in themselves). The failure to draw the distinction between appearances and things in themselves is the hallmark of all those pernicious systems of thought that stand under the title of "transcendental realism".*

In other words, if, as Kant believed, all our knowledge comes to us from experience, but all experience is our experience, it cannot be "pure" experience, because it is mediated by the structure of our minds and our understanding; what we experience is the "phenomena" - that which is provoked in us by the unknowable thing itself - the "noumena".

It is hard to overestimate how profound and far-reaching the consequences of Kant's epistemology have been for Western philosophy and culture. He is saying no one gets to experience outside of his own perceptual experience. One analogy for this is imagining that you had a pair of tinted spectacles that you couldn't ever take off. You might have good reason to believe the world was the colour you were seeing it, but actually because you could never get beyond your spectacles you couldn't see the world as it really was (Kant calls this "Das Ding an sich").

So why is this important for religious experience? The problem for religious believers is that we cannot have a direct (or "noumenal") experience of God or indeed anything. Kant rules out the possibility of any kind of relationship with God, indeed in this system of thought God becomes a mere postulate, an idea he proposes in order to make his system of morality work.

A response to the Kantian problem came from the Romantic movement. While maintaining the same epistemological framework, they bypassed the problem by claiming it was possible to have a pure experience through the operation of the feelings rather than the reason. They especially emphasised intense, visionary or ecstatic experiences as pathways to unmediated reality.

For the Romantics, childhood represented the royal road to these primal ecstatic experiences - as described in Wordsworth's "Prelude", to take just one example. To see why this is the case, we only need to refer to Kant's epistemology - we only learn the tools of understanding that

24

make up our perceptual equipment as we grow, just in the same way we learn how to use our legs to walk. So babies and young children do experience the noumenal world - but they cannot speak of it! The Romantics, then, took the Gospel exhortation "Unless you change utterly and become like a child, you will never enter the Kingdom of Heaven" very seriously!

In the development of this Romantic understanding a key figure is the German theologian **FRIEDRICH SCHLEIERMACHER**. For Schleiermacher the source of religion is a feeling which is prior to consciousness, before the differentiation into subject and object. But what has this to do with William James?

Grace Jantzen summarises the position of Schleiermacher and James:

> *Anglo-American philosophers of religion remain largely untouched by postmodern concerns, and conduct their discussion of mysticism, wittingly or not, under the long shadow of Kant. Central to their definition of mysticism, therefore, is the work of Schleiermacher and William James, who tried to retrieve religious and mystical experience from Kantian strictures by seeing such experiences as unique, intense, subjective states of consciousness occurring "on the verges of the mind" different from normal consciousness and thus escaping Kant's critical theory.*

And she explains Schleiermacher's theory:

> *... immediate consciousness points to the stage before subject and object are differentiated. There is, Schleiermacher suggests, a primal stage of consciousness in any experience, a stage*

before the objective content is discriminated from the subjective participation. This consciousness cannot be consciousness OF anything, it cannot have any specificity, because by the time the object of consciousness has been specified one has already moved away from the primal undifferentiated state. Such movement is of course necessary for thought or knowledge to take place: in this Schleiermacher agrees with Kant. But the truly religious moment is the moment before such differentiation into subject and object has taken place: this is what he means when he speaks of religion as immediate consciousness.

Jantzen also gives six key aspects of Schleiermacher's system:

- Mystical experience consists of pre-rational immediate consciousness or feeling.

- Mystical experience removes the distinction between subject and object.

- Mystical experience is prior to language and is therefore ineffable.

- Mystical experience dissolves or annihilates the self.

- Mystical experience cannot be sustained, and is therefore transient.

- Mystical experience is nevertheless noetic, that is, it imparts insights about the nature of Reality.

At this point it will be obvious even to those who are only slightly familiar with William James how indebted he is to Schleiermacher for his central ideas. James said in Varieties:

> ... *our normal consciousness, rational consciousness as we call it, is but one special type of consciousness whilst all about it, and parted from it by the filmiest of screens, there lie potential forms of consciousness entirely different.*

HEALTHY-MINDEDNESS, THE SICK SOUL, THE DIVIDED SELF AND THE PROCESS OF ITS UNIFICATION, CONVERSION

As a psychologist James is interested in character types, and traces two distinct kinds of religious temperament. The first kind he calls the healthy-minded, which is an essentially optimistic mindset, which places goodness at the forefront of existence and attempts to evade or ignore evil and suffering. He contrasts this with the sick soul type, the pessimist, who sees evil as somehow intrinsic to reality. He comes to this conclusion:

> *The completest religions would therefore seem to be those in which the pessimistic elements are best developed. Buddhism, of course, and Christianity are the best known to us of these. They are essentially religions of deliverance: the man must die to an unreal life before he can be born into the real life.*

When the sick soul is able to be delivered from the depths of its melancholy and suffering, James says that a once-divided self is now able to re-constellate around a new and higher centre of reality - this is the unification of which he speaks, and it forms the basis of what are called conversion experiences. They may be gradual or sudden, but they all have this characteristic quality, that some new centre of energy which transcends the old is found, by which the sick soul is revitalised and finds new moral impetus.

There is then, in this account, a strongly psychological account of conversion experiences, one perhaps reminiscent of Jung, a contemporary psychologist.

JAMES'S CONCLUSIONS

1. That the visible world is part of a more spiritual universe from which it draws its chief significance;

2. That union or harmonious relation with that higher universe is our true end;

3. That prayer or inner communion with the spirit thereof - be that spirit "God" or "law" - is a process wherein work is really done, and spiritual energy flows in and produces effects, psychological or material, within the phenomenal world.

Religion also includes the following psychological characteristics:

4. A new zest which adds itself like a gift to life, and takes the form either of lyrical enchantment or of appeal to earnestness and heroism.

5. "An assurance of safety and a temper of peace, and, in relation to others, a preponderance of loving affections." (From Lecture 20)

Little more really needs to be said here.

EVALUATING WILLIAM JAMES

Now in evaluating James's main aims and conclusions, having taken a detour through the fundamentals which underlie his work, we have some "leverage", some critical heft, which will help us to make salient points.

Let's go back to Kant. While massively influential at the time, his epistemological structure is now strongly contested by academics. But James's theory relies on the notion of "pure" experience, which is part of the Kantian structure. Even though it says there is a way around this Kantian problem, it still accepts as true the Kantian epistemological structure. But what if experience is entirely constructed by language and culture? What if there is no "noumenal" world at all? This is the claim of non-realists such as **DON CUPITT**. In fact non-realism is really only a taking of Kant to its logical conclusion. If you say that there is a noumenal world which it is not possible to know, what actual difference does it make if it doesn't exist at all?

So James doesn't fare very well in a non-realist, postmodern world in which experience is totally constructed. Cupitt has made much of this in his book Mysticism and Modernity. A post-modernist theologian and founder of the "Sea of Faith" movement, Cupitt believes that mystics "create" religious experience by writing about them in profound acts of rebellion against orthodoxy. He points out that many mystics have been highly literary figures - poets like St John of the Cross or the Sufi Rumi, and writers like Teresa of Avila or St Augustine, or Meister Eckhart. Such writing creates the mystical experience for the mystic, and is the primary experience. From this viewpoint there is no pure, culture-neutral religious experience such as James tried to find - language forms events; it goes "all the way down" as Cupitt puts it.

However, there are problems with non-realism, and Cupitt's claim that language entirely constructs experience seems far-fetched to many.

Many philosophers actually subscribe to some form of **CRITICAL REALISM** when it comes to perception, experience and epistemology.

Secondly, a search for a common core, as James attempts to do, is basically an attempt to find some kind of essence to religious experience. But if you accept Wittgenstein's notion of "family resemblance", then there is no "essence" of religious experience - there is simply the different contexts in which religious experience occurs.

Thirdly, there is a problem with ineffability in that a claim is being made that something non-conceptual is happening to an individual, but to have some effect on the person's awareness, there must be some conceptual content to the experience.

MACKIE'S CRITICISMS OF JAMES

In The Miracle of Theism JL Mackie gives a detailed critique of James. He says:

> The verb "to experience" is indeed transitive: any experience must have an object, it must be of something. But it may have an intentional object only, as does a dream experience or the experience of pain. The pain or the dream, will no doubt have causes; but the pain itself has no existence apart from the experience of it, nor do the events which constitute the manifest dream content. Alternatively, an experience may have a real object: we ordinarily suppose our normal perceptual experience to be or to include awareness of independently existing material spatio-temporal things. The question then is whether specifically religious experiences should be taken to have real objects, to give us genuine information about independently existing supernatural entities or spiritual beings, or whether all that matters is their intrinsic character, their intentional objects, and, of course, their influence on the rest of the lives of those who have them.

He questions James's tentative defence of religious experiences' "objective truth":

> Despite James' insistence that the question of the origin of a religious experience is quite distinct from those of its value and truth, there is an important indirect connection between them. Since these experiences are of kinds which are psychologically understandable without the help of any specifically religious

assumptions, they do not in themselves carry any guarantee of a supernatural source.

He says of James,

> *... even what he classes as genuinely religious experiences [ones which leave "good dispositions" in the believer] do not intrinsically resist explanation in purely human terms. This is because today that what was ascribed to the devil in the past can be explained in terms of subconscious motives - purely human desires - so also we can do the same for experiences ascribed to God.*

He concludes that this is fatal for any argument from the experience of God.

> *But surely this is to beg the question of the veridicality of the experience. Just because people now assign to subconscious urges the role that they previously gave to God and the devil, actually doesn't preclude the possibility of the experience being the mark left on our mind by "something more", as James says: "... whatever it may be on its farther side, the 'more' with which in religious experience we feel ourselves connected is on its hither side the subconscious continuation of our conscious life." (Lecture XX)*

As Mackie says, though, it comes down to which is the more plausible hypothesis - and he says that James gives no good reason to believe the theistic one.

He mentions conflicting claims challenges:

Kierkegaard says that one who, living in an idolatrous community, prays to an idol in the right spirit thereby prays, after all, to the true god. But this cuts both ways. It entails that one who prays, intentionally, to a specifically Christian god, and who has an experience as of Christ or the Virgin Mary, may, by the same token, be receiving a response from some quite different true god who is sufficiently broadminded to make allowances for the trivial errors of his worshippers. When the Christian says "I know that my redeemer liveth", we must reply "No, you don't: certainly not if you mean, by 'my redeemer', Jesus as distinct from Osiris or Ashtaroth or Dionysus or Baldur or Vishnu or Amida." But equally the response may be coming from no god beyond the experiencer's own unconscious mind.

Mackie also says:

Religious experience is also essentially incapable of supporting any argument for the traditional central doctrines of theism.

He says James agrees:

... religious experience, as we have studied it, cannot be cited as unequivocally supporting the infinitist belief. The only thing that it unequivocally testifies to is that we can experience union with something larger than ourselves and in that union find our greatest peace ... It need not be infinite. (James VRE p499)

Mackie shows that James's empiricism could lead him to affirm the supernaturalist hypothesis over the hypothesis of naturalism only if it was capable of explaining certain events such as miracles, that naturalism could not.

Finally Mackie says that religious experiences are not self-authenticating:

> *Mystical states, he [James] says, are "absolutely authoritative over the individuals to whom they come"; yet "No authority emanates from them which should make it a duty for those who stand outside of them to accept their revelations uncritically"; nevertheless, "They break down the authority of the non-mystical or rationalistic consciousness, based upon the understanding and the senses alone. They show it to be only one kind of consciousness. They open out the possibility of other orders of truth, in which, so far as anything in us vitally responds to them, we may freely continue to have faith." (p407)*

But this is incoherent. Since, as he rightly says, no authority emanates from mystical experiences - because they can be so easily explained in purely natural, psychological, terms - for anyone who stands outside them to accept their revelations, they cannot be authoritative in an objective sense even for those who have them.

Mackie's criticisms of James are important. They reveal some fundamental issues which seem difficult to resolve on the account that James provides.

SELF-ASSESSMENT QUESTIONS

1. Write a paragraph explaining James's approach to religious experience using the terms "pragmatism", "phenomenological" and "psychological".

2. What are the strengths of taking a phenomenological approach to religious experience?

3. How does James attempt to sidestep the problem posed by Kantian epistemology?

4. To what extent does James succeed in this?

5. Do you agree with James's conclusions? Explain your answer.

6. Explain James's aims in Varieties.

7. How plausible does James's account of conversion experiences seem?

8. Describe the non-realist challenge to James's arguments.

9. Describe Mackie's key criticisms of James.

10. Which of Mackie's criticisms seems strongest to you and why?

FURTHER READING

JAMES, W - The Varieties of Religious Experience

MACKIE, J L - The Miracle of Theism, OUP, 1982 (Chapter 10)

Different forms of religious experience

KEYWORDS

- **AWEFULNESS** - Characteristic of numinous experience, provoking overpowering feelings of awe.

- **CHARISMATIC** - Relating to spiritual power given by God.

- **COGNITIVE** - Capable of truth or falsity.

- **CREATURE-FEELING** - The consciousness of being a creature.

- **NON-COGNITIVE** - Incapable of truth or falsity.

- **NORMATIVE** - Relating to what should occur; prescriptive - often used in the field of ethics.

VISIONS AND VOICES

It could be argued that visions and voices are central to the foundation of Christianity. For it was the vision of St Paul of the risen Christ on the road to Damascus, as well as the voice that he heard speaking to him, that provided the impetus for all the subsequent work of St Paul in spreading the Gospel around the Mediterranean:

> *As [Saul] neared Damascus on his journey, suddenly a light from heaven flashed around him. He fell to the ground and heard a*

voice say to him, "Saul, Saul, why do you persecute me?" (Acts 9:3-4)

And it was the voice heard by St Augustine, which prompted him to read the Bible, which was instrumental in his conversion and thus shaped the intellectual and doctrinal development of Christianity for nearly two millennia:

Suddenly a voice reaches my ears from a nearby house. It is the voice of a boy or girl (I don't know which) and in a kind of singsong the words are constantly repeated: "Take it and read it. Take it and read it." At once my face changed ... I could not remember that I had heard anything like it before. (Confessions)

Visions or appearances are also fundamental to the disciples' experience at the first Easter - the appearances of the risen Christ are numerous. Clearly they are vision-like in that sometimes Christ appears suddenly in a locked room (John), or he is not at first recognised. Some of them, however, might be said to go beyond visions into actual encounters - for example Thomas actually puts his hands into the wounds of Christ.

Visions have been a part of the religious experiences of great mystics like St Teresa of Avila. Speaking of "intellectual visions", she says:

... a person who is in no way expecting such a favour nor has ever imagined herself worthy of receiving it, is conscious that Jesus Christ stands by her side although she sees Him neither with the eyes of the body nor of the soul.

This is called an intellectual vision; I cannot tell why. I knew a person to whom God granted both this grace and others I shall describe later on. At first it distressed her, for she could not understand it; she could see nothing, yet so convinced did she feel that Jesus Christ was thus in some way manifesting Himself that she could not doubt that it was some kind of vision, whether it came from God or no. Its powerful effects were a strong argument that it was from Him; still she was alarmed, never having heard of an intellectual vision, nor was she aware that such a thing could be. She however felt certain of our Lord's presence, and He spoke to her several times in the way that I described. Before she had received this favour, she had heard words spoken but had never known who uttered them.

Teresa contrasts such "intellectual visions" with imaginary visions, saying that the former do not pass away quickly like the latter, but last for days.

Apparitions of the Virgin Mary, such as those which happened to Bernadette at Lourdes, or to the three peasant children, Lucia, Jacinta and Francisco, might also be classed as visions, although the latter would differ in that it could be seen by more than one person, whereas only Bernadette ever saw her visions of Mary.

Questions about what exactly an intellectual vision is have been posed by philosophers. Some have considered that a vision that is not really seen but only sensed might be more akin to an intuition - a knowing that someone is present.

Voices and conversion

Here is an excerpt from Lecture XI of The Varieties of Religious Experience which quotes from **EDWIN STARBUCK**, who did much research into the psychology of religion. The context of this passage is the effect of religious experience on behaviour, particularly its ability to effect sudden and permanent cures for addictive behaviour. He cites two examples of people hearing the "voice of God" and subsequently turning from destructive behaviour. He links such cures with the effect hypnosis can have on addiction, and concludes that if the grace of God is working it probably works through this subliminal (unconscious) pathway.

A good way to approach a question on voices, then, would be not to try and deal with them only in isolation, but consider them, as James did, in the light of their effect on conversion. This gives you much wider scope to talk about psychological influences, and bring in far more of Varieties:

Here is an analogous case from Starbuck's manuscript collection:

"I went into the old Adelphi Theatre, where there was a Holiness meeting ... and I began saying, 'Lord, Lord, I must have this blessing.' Then what was to me an audible voice said: 'Are you willing to give up everything to the Lord?' and question after question kept coming up, to all of which I said: 'Yes, Lord; yes, Lord!' until this came: 'Why do you not accept it now?' and I said: 'I do, Lord.' - I felt no particular joy, only a trust. Just then the meeting closed, and, as I went out on the street, I met a gentleman smoking a fine cigar, and a cloud of smoke came into my face, and I took a long, deep breath of it, and praise the Lord, all my appetite for it was gone. Then as I walked along the street, passing saloons where the fumes of liquor came out, I found that all my taste and longing for that accursed stuff was gone. Glory to God! ... [But] for ten or eleven long years [after that] I was in the

wilderness with its ups and downs. My appetite for liquor never came back."

"The classic case of Colonel Gardiner is that of a man cured of sexual temptation in a single hour. To Mr. Spears the colonel said, 'I was effectually cured of all inclination to that sin I was so strongly addicted to that I thought nothing but shooting me through the head could have cured me of it; and all desire and inclination to it was removed, as entirely as if I had been a sucking child; nor did the temptation return to this day.' Mr. Webster's words on the same subject are these: 'One thing I have heard the colonel frequently say, that he was much addicted to impurity before his acquaintance with religion; but that, so soon as he was enlightened from above, he felt the power of the Holy Ghost changing his nature so wonderfully that his sanctification in this respect seemed more remarkable than in any other.'*

*Doddridge's Life of Colonel James Gardiner, London Religious Tract Society, pp23-32.

Such rapid abolition of ancient impulses and propensities reminds us so strongly of what has been observed as the result of hypnotic suggestion that it is difficult not to believe that subliminal influences play the decisive part in these abrupt changes of heart, just as they do in hypnotism.*

* Here, for example, is a case, from Starbuck's book, in which a "sensory automatism" brought about quickly what prayers and resolves had been unable to effect. The subject is a woman. She writes:

"When I was about forty I tried to quit smoking, but the desire was on me, and had me in its power. I cried and

*prayed and promised God to quit, but could not. I had
smoked for fifteen years. When I was fifty three, as I sat by
the fire one day smoking, a voice came to me. I did not
hear it with my ears, but more as a dream or sort of double
think. It said, 'Louisa, lay down smoking.' At once I replied,
'Will you take the desire away?' But it only kept saying:
'Louisa, lay down smoking.' Then I got up, laid my pipe on
the mantel-shelf, and never smoked again or had any
desire to. The desire was gone as though I had never
known it or touched tobacco. The sight of others smoking
and the smell of smoke never gave me the least wish to
touch it again." The Psychology of Religion, p142.*

*Suggestive therapeutics abound in records of cure, after a few sittings,
of inveterate bad habits with which the patient, left to ordinary moral
and physical influences, had struggled in vain. Both drunkenness and
sexual vice have been cured in this way, action through the subliminal
seeming thus in many individuals to have the prerogative of inducing
relatively stable change. If the grace of God miraculously operates, it
probably operates through the subliminal door, then. But just how
anything operates in this region is still unexplained, and we shall do
well now to say good-by to the process of transformation altogether -
leaving it, if you like, a good deal of a psychological or theological
mystery - and to turn our attention to the fruits of the religious
condition, no matter in what way they may have been produced.***

> *** Professor Starbuck expresses the radical destruction of
> old influences physiologically, as a cutting off of the
> connection between higher and lower cerebral centres.
> "This condition," he says, "in which the association-
> centres connected with the spiritual life are cut off from the
> lower, is often reflected in the way correspondents describe*

their experiences ... For example: 'Temptations from without still assail me, but there is nothing within to respond to them.' The ego [here] is wholly identified with the higher centres, whose quality of feeling is that of withinness. Another of the respondents says: 'Since then, although Satan tempts me, there is as it were a wall of brass around me, so that his darts cannot touch me.'" - Unquestionably, functional exclusions of this sort must occur in the cerebral organ. But on the side accessible to introspection, their causal condition is nothing but the degree of spiritual excitement, getting at last so high and strong as to be sovereign; and it must be frankly confessed that we do not know just why or how such sovereignty comes about in one person and not in another. We can only give our imagination a certain delusive help by mechanical analogies.

"If we should conceive, for example, that the human mind, with its different possibilities of equilibrium, might be like a many-sided solid with different surfaces on which it could lie flat, we might liken mental revolutions to the spatial revolutions of such a body. As it is pried up, say by a lever, from a position in which it lies on surface A, for instance, it will linger for a time unstably halfway up, and if the lever cease to urge it, it will tumble back or "relapse" under the continued pull of gravity. But if at last it rotate far enough for its centre of gravity to pass beyond surface A altogether, the body will fall over, on surface B, say, and abide there permanently. The pulls of gravity towards A have vanished, and may now be disregarded. The

polyhedron has become immune against farther attraction from their direction.

"In this figure of speech the lever may correspond to the emotional influence making for a new life, and the initial pull of gravity to the ancient drawbacks and inhibitions. So long as the emotional influence fails to reach a certain pitch of efficacy, the changes it produces are unstable, and the man relapses into his original attitude. But when a certain intensity is attained by the new emotion, a critical point is passed, and there then ensues an irreversible revolution, equivalent to the production of a new nature.

"The collective name for the ripe fruits of religion in a character is Saintliness.* The saintly character is the character for which spiritual emotions are the habitual centre of the personal energy; and there is a certain composite photograph of universal saintliness, the same in all religions, of which the features can easily be traced."

We can see in these last paragraphs how James formulates his theory of conversion, once again giving primary importance to feeling, which acts "as a lever". Of course, James's empiricism struggles with his desire to give these experiences their due here, and he merely pushes back the question of the veridicality of an experience into the psychological sphere. "Religious feeling" is conveniently acceptable as a psychological phenomenon, without enquiring too closely into what it is we can have a naturalistic account of conversion. But his account is still persuasive. Undoubtedly it accords with the insights of virtue ethics, and much of modern psychological understanding about habitual behaviour.

Indeed, Alcoholics Anonymous' 12-step programme for recovering from alcohol dependence recognises the importance of acceptance of a higher power into the alcoholic's life. The programme, reproduced below, can clearly be seen as larger than just stopping addiction:

1. We admitted we were powerless over alcohol - that our lives had become unmanageable.

2. Came to believe that a power greater than ourselves could restore us to sanity.

3. Made a decision to turn our will and our lives over to the care of God as we understood Him.

4. Made a searching and fearless moral inventory of ourselves.

5. Admitted to God, to ourselves, and to another human being the exact nature of our wrongs.

6. Were entirely ready to have God remove all these defects of character.

7. Humbly asked Him to remove our shortcomings.

8. Made a list of all persons we had harmed, and became willing to make amends to them all.

9. Made direct amends to such people wherever possible, except when to do so would injure them or others.

10. Continued to take personal inventory, and when we were wrong, promptly admitted it.

11. Sought through prayer and meditation to improve our conscious contact with God as we understood Him, praying only for knowledge of His will for us and the power to carry that out.

12. Having had a spiritual awakening as the result of these steps, we tried to carry this message to alcoholics, and to practice these principles in all our affairs.

There is here a strong pragmatic argument for the acceptance of some kind of religious experience involving conversion, or turning away from destructive patterns in a person's life. Many people would testify to the importance of psychological readiness to accept outside help from a higher power, and its effect in transforming people's lives.

However, critics may argue that this is just a psychological technique, a self-help tool, rather than a meaningful turning to God.

NUMINOUS EXPERIENCE

In The Idea of The Holy **RUDOLF OTTO** characterises religious experiences as feelings of dependence, awe-inspiring, fascinating and terrifying.

Otto was one of the most influential thinkers about religion in the first half of the 20th C. He is best known for his analysis of the experience that, in his view, underlies all religion. He calls this experience "numinous", and says it has three components. These are often designated with a Latin phrase: "mysterium tremendum et fascinans". As "mysterium", the numinous is "wholly other" - entirely different from anything we experience in ordinary life. It evokes a reaction of silence. But the numinous is also a "mysterium tremendum". It provokes terror because it presents itself as overwhelming power. Finally, the numinous presents itself as "fascinans", as merciful and gracious.

Outline of Otto's concept of the numinous

(Based on The Idea of the Holy, trans. John W Harvey; Oxford: Oxford University Press, 1923; 2nd ed, 1950 [Das Heilige, 1917])

MYSTERIUM TREMENDUM ET FASCINANS - Fearful and fascinating mystery.

MYSTERIUM - Wholly Other, experienced with blank wonder, stupor.

TREMENDUM - Awefulness, terror, demonic dread, awe, absolute unapproachability, "wrath" of God, overpoweringness, majesty, might, sense of one's own nothingness in contrast to its power, creature-feeling, sense of objective presence, dependence, energy, urgency, will, vitality.

FASCINANS - Potent charm, attractiveness in spite of fear, terror, etc.

Examples are numerous, especially Old Testament ones. For example, Ezekiel's vision of the Seraphim - he found himself indescribably insignificant and sinful in comparison to the majesty of the vision.

The term numinous is derived from the Latin word "numen", meaning "divine power". The numinous really refers to the non-rational element of religion, which is properly the object of mysticism. The concepts of religion, the doctrines and moral codes, are the rational element, which according to Otto derive ultimately from the non-rational numinous element.

Otto describes the feeling, which he calls the "mysterium tremendum":

> *This feeling may at times come sweeping like a gentle tide, pervading the mind with a tranquil mood of deepest worship. It may pass over into a more set and lasting attitude of the soul, continuing, as it were, thrillingly vibrant and resonant ... It may burst in sudden eruption up from the depths of the soul with spasms and convulsions, or lead to the strangest excitements, to intoxicated frenzy, to transport, and to ecstasy.*

There are some useful passages in children's literature which help to describe this concept. Take this scene from The Wind in the Willows by Kenneth Grahame:

> *"This is the place of my song-dream, the place the music played to me," whispered the Rat, as if in a trance. "Here, in this holy place, here if anywhere, surely we shall find Him!"*

Then suddenly the Mole felt a great Awe fall upon him, an awe that turned his muscles to water, bowed his head, and rooted his feet to the ground. It was no panic terror - indeed he felt wonderfully at peace and happy - but it was an awe that smote and held him and, without seeing, he knew it could only mean that some august Presence was very, very near. With difficulty he turned to look for his friend. and saw him at his side cowed, stricken, and trembling violently. And still there was utter silence in the populous bird-haunted branches around them; and still the light grew and grew.

Or take this passage from The Lion, the Witch and the Wardrobe by CS Lewis:

At the name of Aslan each one of the children felt something jump in his inside.

None of the children knew who Aslan was ... but the moment the Beaver had spoken these words everyone felt quite different. Perhaps it has sometimes happened to you in a dream that someone says something which you don't understand but in the dream it feels as if it had some enormous meaning ... so beautiful that you remember it all your life.

The element of **AWEFULNESS** associated with certain places (such as the riverbank in The Wind in the Willows) or names (such as the name of Aslan) can be clearly seen in Judeo-Christian scriptures. For instance, the commandment by God to Moses "Remove your sandals, for you stand on holy ground" in Exodus 3:5 expresses this attitude of reverence and fear appropriate to the numinous. Equally, in Christian worship we see expressions of the numinous. Otto singles out the words from the Gloria in Christian liturgy: "For you alone are the Holy One, you alone are the Lord, you alone are the Most High ..."

The element of absolute otherness associated with the numinous leads to the experience of "creature-feeling" in the worshipper, where the overpowering element of the numinous causes us to experience our own feeling of dependence, that we are mere creatures, "submerged and overwhelmed by our own nothingness in contrast to that which is supreme above all creatures".

This notion of "creature-feeling" is clearly influenced by Schleiermacher's "feeling of absolute dependence", but Otto is keen to distinguish the two from each other. Schleiermacher meant by his term the feeling of contingency dependent on being the creation of a creator. Otto argues that the conceptualisation of overpoweringness in terms of a causal relationship between creator and created misses out an important aspect of the numinous experience. He says:

> In one case you have the fact of being created; in the other, the status of the creature ... with this latter type of consciousness, we are introduced to a set of ideas quite different to those of creation or preservation. We come upon the ideas, first, of the annihilation of self, and then, as its complement, of the transcendent as the sole and entire reality.

Essentially Otto believes that the numinous, at its base, goes beyond the feelings of trust and love of Schleiermacher's analysis into a non-rational sphere that occupies the entire being with a bewildering strength. "If a man does not feel what the numinous is, when he reads the sixth chapter of Isaiah, then no 'preaching, singing, telling', in Luther's phrase, can avail him," Otto writes.

Therefore the numinous experience is ineffable, and indeed the Via Negativa of the mystics may be a particularly useful way of trying to grasp what Otto means for the student who has completed the Religious Language topic.

Issues related to the numinous

▶ **The primacy of feeling**

William James claims: "Feeling is the deeper source of religion … philosophic and theological formulas are secondary." It is easy to see the connections between Otto and James - both put feeling at the centre of their theories. We have already traced the journey of such an attempt back through the Romantics to Schleiermacher. I would suggest that much good work can be done in this topic by contrasting this modern attempt to base an argument on religious experience through the emphasis on the emotive aspect with more ancient theories from within theistic traditions themselves, for instance, the Church Fathers have much to say on this topic, as does the Orthodox tradition. Aquinas, Aristotle and Plato could all be fruitfully used as a contrast.

All of these more ancient traditions make use of theories of the soul that go back to the Greek philosophers, wherein the soul was essentially divided into a higher rational part (called the **LOGISTIKON**) and a lower irrational part (**ALOGON**). This irrational part was divided into desires and aggression and was known collectively as the passionate part. This lower part dealt with the world as presented by the senses, which is how the passions were able to enter into the soul and cloud its ability to see God. The individual soul met with God at the apex of the higher part of the soul (you could call it the domain of the spirit). This was possible because there was a distinction in the higher part between intellect and reason. Reason was that capacity of mind which worked with the senses to quantify and analyse the natural world, whereas the intellect was the capacity to come to an awareness of the unseen worlds above the physical one. Here we can quote **JOSEF PIEPER**:

> *The medievals distinguished between the intellect as ratio and the intellect as intellectus. Ratio is the power of discursive thought, of searching and re-searching, abstracting, refining, and concluding [cf. Latin dis-currere, 'to run to and fro'], whereas intellectus refers to the ability of 'simply looking' (simplex intuitus), to which the truth presents itself as a landscape presents itself to the eye. The spiritual knowing power of the human mind, as the ancients understood it, is really two things in one: ratio and intellectus, all knowing involves both.*

It is clear from this simple outline that religious experience is traditionally thought of not as non-rational and feeling-based, but as supra-rational, ie going beyond or above the rational into the domain of the intellect, where the truth is presented to one.

It may be helpful to use these distinctions when discussing James and Otto's work, as their theories are sometimes not dealt with carefully enough by students who claim that for them religious experience is just a feeling. It is possible to reconcile James and Otto with these ancient traditions if we bear in mind this distinction between ratio and intellectus. After all, Otto shows very clearly that his **CREATURE-FEELING** "holy fear" and "awe" are firstly the effect left on the soul of the person, and not the experience itself, and secondly that they are qualitatively different from ordinary "feeling" as we would know it. For instance, the discussion in The Idea of the Holy about the fear the disciples have of the storm contrasted with the fear they have of Jesus when he calms the storm. The words used are different - the calming of the storm brings a kind of holy fear.

If the intellect is defined as the core of one's being rather than one's understanding then we have a way of seeing the experience as an encounter with God at the depths of one's soul, which would be shattering for the rational and emotional parts of the soul.

▸ **Can we claim that numinous experiences are veridical - that they are an insight into the divine?**

The sceptic might claim they are just feelings, perhaps more intense than others but still understandable psychologically.

However, this doesn't help very much - many feelings are based on judgements and dependent on interpretations of situations. For example, feelings of contempt towards those we have seen acting badly. In other words, emotion is never purely internal - it is linked to the external world, so the fact that the numinous has an emotional content doesn't mean there is no reality behind it.

▸ **Are numinous experiences cognitive or non-cognitive?**

RW Hepburn draws parallels with other experiences such as the motion of the sea still felt even when the ship stops moving. He says that it is hard to decide if this feeling is real or imagined, but we can always check whether we are still on the ship or not. With numinous experience there is nothing to help us to decide. He concludes it is probably impossible to answer the question of whether they are **COGNITIVE** or **NON-COGNITIVE**.

There are also similarities with types of aesthetic experience, such as hearing a symphony and being moved or transported; feelings of the sublime in nature, cathartic release of emotions from viewing drama and so on. Some might appeal to the comparison to lend weight to the veridicality of numinous experience. We know we cannot put our experience of Beethoven's Fifth Symphony into words – we don't disbelieve in it because we cannot do this - so we shouldn't with numinous experience.

Unfortunately this still begs the question - cognitive or non-cognitive? Why say numinous experience is experience of a "Wholly Other" realm? We don't usually believe the same for the musical experience.

CORPORATE EXPERIENCE

Corporate experiences are those undergone by a group of people. They might take the form of miraculous experiences like the perception of the Sun "dancing" by a large group of people in Fatima, Portugal in 1917, or at the other end of the scale, group experiences of peacefulness and calm during periods of silence during, for example, Quaker meetings. There are also what would be called "charismatic" experiences such as the Toronto Blessing, a group experience in Toronto Airport chapel in 1994 in which various phenomena were reported among the congregation. These included laughter, falling over, crying, shaking uncontrollably, roaring, a feeling of intoxicating joy, and experiences of being uncoordinated.

On the face of it, it seems that only the most naive and uncritical could accept group experiences like the Toronto Blessing as veridical in an age in which the social sciences have developed sophisticated accounts of the behaviour of groups of people which explain the peculiarities without recourse to religious causes. The most common explanation in these terms is known as crowd or mob psychology. People act differently in groups, become more suggestible and open to unusual patterns of behaviour. In these "charismatic" gatherings there may also be those present who are actively seeking such experiences. If we apply Teresa of Avila's criteria to this, when she says that humility is a pre-requisite for any religious experience - the soul must not even think itself worthy of such blessings - we can see the strongest possible contrast with the words of the preacher behind the Toronto Blessings, Rodney Howard Browne, who said: "God, if you don't come down here and touch me, I'm going to come up there and touch you!"

How can we not also be aware of the lessons of the 20th C, which has been called the age of the masses - when it comes to an awareness of the strange ways people in large groups can behave? Carl Jung talks about the waves of unconscious psychic content which broke out across Europe between the wars; he talks of the "thin veneer of civilisation" under which humans are frighteningly close to earlier "savage" behaviour. So the fact that some groups of people, who are already suggestible and open to "charismatic" phenomena, experience such things is perhaps not entirely surprising.

But should we dismiss all such corporate experiences out of hand? If we are willing to suspend judgement for a few moments, from a sheer numerical point of view aren't the experiences more persuasive than individual ones? Crowd psychology also often results in more negative behaviour - these experiences are generally positive. And what about the biblical basis of such experiences?

The key text for charismatic style experiences is from Acts 2 - the description of Pentecost:

> *When the day of Pentecost had come, they were all together in one place. And suddenly from heaven there came a sound like the rush of a violent wind, and it filled the entire house where they were sitting. Divided tongues, as of fire, appeared among them, and a tongue rested on each of them. All of them were filled with the Holy Spirit and began to speak in other languages, as the Spirit gave them ability.*

> *5 Now there were devout Jews from every nation under heaven living in Jerusalem. And at this sound the crowd gathered and was bewildered, because each one heard them speaking in the native language of each. Amazed and astonished, they asked, "Are not all these who are speaking Galileans? And how is it*

that we hear, each of us, in our own native language? Parthians, Medes, Elamites, and residents of Mesopotamia, Judea and Cappadocia, Pontus and Asia, Phrygia and Pamphylia, Egypt and the parts of Libya belonging to Cyrene, and visitors from Rome, both Jews and proselytes, Cretans and Arabs - in our own languages we hear them speaking about God's deeds of power." All were amazed and perplexed, saying to one another, "What does this mean?" But others sneered and said, "They are filled with new wine."

This is an experience which is called "speaking in tongues" or **GLOSSOLALIA**. Many have pointed out that in charismatic worship much of what is called "speaking in tongues" is actually not understandable by anyone, unlike the biblical version. What is interesting though, is that people thought the disciples were drunk. Would they necessarily have thought that if they were only speaking lots of different languages? Possibly it might have sounded like drunken babble if you didn't understand it, but could it also be that some of the other types of effect like being uncoordinated and falling over, laughing and so on which are associated with the Toronto Blessing style of experience might have occurred?

Also cited in support of these kind of corporate experiences are the historical occurrences. As far back as John Wesley, experiences of holy laughter and other charismatic phenomena were occurring during worship, although it seems John Wesley was mistrustful of holy laughter, believing it to be of the devil.

I think this is probably many people's initial reaction to some of the more extreme manifestations of "charismatic" experiences - certainly there are many evangelical Churches who think the animal noises, roaring and holy laughter of the Toronto Blessing are actually diabolical experiences from the devil.

Some tests have been proposed, in line with the venerable tradition: "By their fruits shall they be judged". Do the congregation who regularly experience holy laughter and other group manifestations of the "spirit" experience more harmonious relations with each other as a result? Do they experience a desire to know Christ more deeply through scriptural study and good works? If the answer to these questions is in the negative, and if there is a self-indulgent tendency to seek more charismatic experiences, then one might be more sceptical about the corporate experience. Many Christians might also apply the words from John's Gospel: "Beloved, do not believe every spirit, but test the spirits, whether they are of God; because many false prophets have gone out into the world." (I John 4:1)

Perhaps the last word on the Toronto Blessings should go to a Christian pastor, Gino Geraci:

> The apostles John and Paul both indicate experiences with God of surpassing depth and richness, from seeing the heavens opened to being "caught up into the third heaven". Paul urged all believers to "eagerly desire the greater gifts", especially that they might prophesy, or tell forth the truth of God. But neither Paul nor John held their own experience to be normative for the Church. Neither urged Christians to seek the personal, subjective experience that they had had. In 1 Corinthians 14, Paul indicates that Tongues is a minor gift and a personal, rather than corporate, experience, and that we should seek rather to edify the Body by that which is intelligible. All such "experiences" are just that, "experiences", personal and subjective. Since there is

no Biblical "experience" beyond salvation and sanctification which is normative for all believers, all other "spiritual experiences" are to be in the background of our corporate expression. The attitude we find expressed by the apostles concerning such experiences is one of humility and submission to the common good. The article, however, quotes Howard-Browne as saying, "either You come down here and touch me, or I will come up there and touch You".

Overall, for the charismatic style experience, the psychological explanation seems very persuasive, even given their widespread nature and possible biblical basis.

SELF-ASSESSMENT QUESTIONS

1. Find one example of each of the following: visions, voices, conversion experience, numinous experience and corporate experience, using the internet or The Varieties of Religious Experience, and briefly describe it.

2. How are visions different from hallucinations? What tests might there be to distinguish the two?

3. Does it make a difference if the voice Augustine heard was an actual child's voice or a "spiritual voice"?

4. To what extent do psychological explanations work for conversion experiences?

5. Create a mind map on numinous experience using the terms "mysterium", "tremendum" and "fascinans" as a structure.

6. To what extent is numinous experience non-cognitive?

7. How do numinous experiences differ from mystical experiences? What are the similarities?

8. "Corporate experiences are weaker evidence for the existence of God than individual experiences." Discuss.

9. Google "holy laughter", "glossolalia" and "charismatic", and watch some videos relating to them. Describe your reaction to them.

10. To what extent do things like Persinger's Helmet weaken arguments for the veridicality of religious experience?

FURTHER READING

OTTO, R - The Idea of the Holy, OUP, 1958

PETERSON et al. - Reason and Religious Belief, OUP 2003 (Chapter 2)

JACKSON, R - The God of Philosophy, 2nd ed., Acumen, 2011 (Chapter 6)

The cognitive status of religious experience - Swinburne's argument

KEY WORDS

- **AXIOMATIC** - Describing an assumption made for the sake of an argument; a universal, self-evident truth.

- **LOGICAL GAP OBJECTION** - Also known as the certitude/certainty distinction - the gap between feeling sure that an experience is veridical, and it being veridical.

- **OCKHAM'S RAZOR** - Principle that states that in a situation where two competing theories both fit the facts, the hypothesis that assumes the least (or is the least complex) should be chosen. Also known as the law of parsimony.

- **PRIMA FACIE** - On the face of it; at first sight. (Latin)

RICHARD SWINBURNE (1934-2005) in his book The Existence of God, presents a cumulative case argument for theism ("On our total evidence theism is more probable than not"). He defends this claim by analysing several arguments, assessing their explanatory power, finding the theistic hypothesis to be persuasive on the basis of its simplicity, but not finding any one argument to be particularly strong. However, Swinburne argues that presented together, these arguments, in spite of their flaws, raise the background probability of theism above an improbable level. They don't establish anything beyond that though, and this is where Swinburne uses religious experience. He claims that the sheer weight of examples of religious experience tips the balance of probability in favour of theism.

But to do this he has to make a case for religious experience as veridical. It is no good having lots of testimony for something if that thing turns out to be an illusion. How does he get round the sceptical challenge to religious experience? He turns the tables on the sceptic. This is an important move, and we shall examine it in detail.

Swinburne's definition of religious experience is:

> ... an experience which seems to the subject to be an experience of God (either of his just being there, or doing or bringing about something) or of some other supernatural thing.

The important thing to notice in his definition is his emphasis on the subject's perception - what seems to be the case. (We shall need to examine whether the emphasis on the analogy to perception is appropriate for religious experience. It is an emphasis that has been made by many modern philosophers, but there have been different emphases, for instance religious experience as an intuition of value or beauty.) This focus on what seems to be the case gives him the principles underlying his argument.

THE PRINCIPLE OF CREDULITY

This states that we ought to believe that things are as they seem to be unless we have evidence that we are mistaken.

Swinburne notes two very different uses of such words as "looks", "seems" and "appears"; one use he calls the **EPISTEMIC** sense, and the other the **COMPARATIVE** sense. Essentially the epistemic sense is what we believe to be the case based on what we experience, eg when we look at a coin from an angle and say "it looks round", whereas the comparative sense describes the way things seem by comparing them with the way things normally seem, eg when we look at a coin from an angle and say "it looks elliptical".

He makes this distinction to highlight the way he is going to use the word "seem" in the Principle of Credulity.

Many people have reported experiences that seem to them unmistakably to be personal encounters with a power greater than themselves (see the David Hay research in the Introduction). This is clearly an epistemic use of the word seem - based on the knowledge of personal encounters a person has, they infer the personal nature of that which has been experienced. I know what it is to experience the love and kindness of others in close relationships; analogically then, my religious experience seemed to be that kind of experience, but magnified in the degree of intensity.

Swinburne says that this Principle of Credulity is a basic principle of rationality; in other words, it is almost **AXIOMATIC**. And it does seem to be the case that we have to presume this principle in our daily lives in order to get along at all. It underlies most of the way we interact with the world. If we maintained a radical scepticism about what our senses seemed to be telling us we would get stuck in a sceptical bog; become paralysed by doubt. We just have to accept the evidence of our senses most of the time. Swinburne is saying, why does the sceptic or atheist make an exception to this principle as soon as something "religious" is experienced? Surely this is mere prejudice?

> *If you say the contrary - never trust appearances until it is proved that they are reliable - you will never have any beliefs at all. For what would show that appearances are reliable, except more appearances? And, if you cannot trust appearances as such, you cannot trust these new ones either. Just as you must trust your five ordinary senses, so it is equally rational to trust your religious sense. (Is There a God?, p132)*

This is an important answer to what is called the **LOGICAL GAP OBJECTION** to religious experience.

It should be recognised that Swinburne's argument actually relies on principles other than just the Principle of Credulity. Some of these others are more implicit within his argument but just as important:

THE PRINCIPLE OF TESTIMONY - Other things being equal, others' experiences are likely to be as they report them to be.

THE PRINCIPLE OF SIMPLICITY - "In a given field, we take as most likely to be true the simplest theory which fits best with other theories of neighbouring fields to produce the simplest set of theories of the world."

THE PRINCIPLE OF CHARITY - Other things being equal, we suppose that other people are like ourselves.

We shall examine the first of these in more detail below, as it is importantly connected to the Principle of Credulity. These other principles employed in Swinburne's argument have the crucial function of broadening out what may seem rather naive and egocentric if the Principle of Credulity is taken alone. They allow for the social dimension of knowing wherein others' perceptions count (the Principle of Testimony). They also show that for this kind of procedure, some rational principles are needed in order to sift through the data; just lots of experiences and testimonies alone will never be enough.

The Principle of Simplicity is just such a rational principle, and is key to Swinburne's argument - it provides the foundation for his cumulative case argument, and it also shows what would be counter evidence to a prima facie claim of justification:

> We should not believe that things are as they seem to be in cases when such a belief is in conflict with the simplest theory compatible with a vast number of data obtained by supposing in a vast number of other cases that things are as they seem to be.

This is really a version of what is known as **OCKHAM'S RAZOR**, or the **LAW OF PARSIMONY**, which states that where there are competing theories, the one with the fewest assumptions should be selected. There are important consequences to this. Swinburne has provided a kind of filter by which we can check the validity of the experience without needing the kind of externally verifiable checks that perceptual experience is often supposed to provide for religious experience.

OBJECTIONS TO THE PRINCIPLE OF CREDULITY

Students often make the mistake of presuming that Swinburne is proposing some kind of naive trust in appearances which forgets about things like illusions, or that his principle only applies to situations where we can check our experience against others. But Swinburne has anticipated these challenges.

The first challenge - that people can hallucinate while influenced physiologically or chemically - would come under evidence that we are mistaken.

The second challenge - that of corroboration - we have already raised in the introduction and elsewhere (see the Logical Gap Objection). With ordinary senses we can check them to see if they agree with the senses of other people, but religious senses often disagree with the sense of others (they cannot see what you can). Swinburne answers this by saying that the rational person applies the Principle of Credulity before he knows what other people experience. And if there is another observer who corroborates what you have sensed, you later still have to trust your own memory that the observer agreed with you (ie what it seemed to you that the other person said) without present corroboration.

In other words we cannot get away from some form of the Principle of Credulity or trust in what we experience. But this is not all. Swinburne says that religious experiences often do coincide with many other people's in a general awareness of a higher power (we have already seen the percentage could be as high as 40% of the population), and that the most likely explanation for why not everyone can see them is that they are blind to religious realities. He states that if you had three eyewitnesses who claimed to see someone and three who didn't, you would most likely conclude that the three who didn't hadn't noticed the person, rather than that the three who did were mistaken.

So Swinburne's method is the clever one of asking why we make an exception to an axiomatic principle of rationality when it comes to religion. He then goes on to extend this principle to the reporting of religious experience, which leads us to the second principle.

THE PRINCIPLE OF TESTIMONY

Again a basic principle of rationality, claims Swinburne, is that those who do not have an experience of a certain type ought to believe others when they say that they do (again barring evidence which would make us disbelieve them - eg that they are a known habitual liar). Again, if we didn't follow this principle of rationality, Swinburne says, we would have almost non-existent knowledge of geography, history or science. The principle of testimony is a kind of applying of the Principle of Credulity to the experiences of other people.

Swinburne next moves on to examining the conditions under which we would not trust what seemed to us to be the case, in order to see if religious experiences usually occur under these conditions. He concludes that usually religious experiences don't occur under these conditions.

Three kinds of evidence which count against an experience

First, the experience was made under conditions in which we have evidence that the experience is unreliable, eg reading a book from 100 metres away. We know that this is not possible for the unaided eye because we can use our own eyes to check. Similarly, perceptual experiences under the influence of LSD are seen to be unreliable, as they can be checked and discounted by those not on the drug. Swinburne concludes that most religious experiences are not made under conditions where there is evidence that the experience is unreliable.

Secondly, if an experience conflicts with our background knowledge about the way the world works. Swinburne says:

... with religious experiences: if we have strong reason to suppose that there is no God, we ought to disregard our religious experiences as hallucinatory. But, in so far as the other evidence is ambiguous or counts against but not strongly against the existence of God, our experience (our own or that of many others) ought to tip the balance in favour of God. (Richard Swinburne, Is There a God?, p135)

Thirdly, if the experience was not caused by the object purportedly experienced - eg if you think you see someone when out shopping, but it turns out to be their twin sister. Swinburne says this could only be shown if it can be shown that there is no God. He claims that if there is a God this doesn't happen because God would be behind all the processes that might bring experiences of God about, as he would sustain all physical phenomena.

Someone might claim that fasting brings about visions of God. But if there is a God he could make fasting causally responsible for bringing experiences of him about. Swinburne says that a drug introduced into my eyes may either cause me to see what is not there, or to open my eyes to what is there. If there is a God, it is the latter that happens.

So all Swinburne is really saying is that evidence of the third kind is ultimately a matter of showing that God doesn't exist, which would be down to arguments beyond the scope of religious experience. Remember, Swinburne has already built a cumulative case argument which he thinks is enough to make it probable that God exists, even in the face of challenges such as the problem of evil.

CRITICISMS OF SWINBURNE'S ARGUMENT

We now need to examine his principles to see if they are persuasive. Swinburne is attempting to move the burden of proof to those who doubt religious experiences are veridical. In this respect his project is similar to William Alston, who claims that all beliefs based on perception are **PRIMA FACIE** justified. Swinburne uses similar terminology: he says religious experiences have prima facie evidential force. We shall hear more about this later. Firstly, I want to examine Swinburne's treatment of the three kinds of evidence against religious experience.

Swinburne's first kind of evidence which would work against the Principle of Credulity is when it occurs under conditions which make it unreliable, such as under the influence of LSD. Is it clear that most religious experiences don't occur under such conditions? Not if we include the many occasions where the use of psychoactive plants are used by individuals - often called shamans - in traditional cultures to give access to the sacred realm. Either Swinburne has to conclude that these experiences are all hallucinatory, or narrow his definition of religious experience. It may be tempting to argue that they are hallucinations, but he has already said that drugs may cause one to open one's eyes to what is already there, which appears to conflict with this first type of evidence.

Would Swinburne also have to discount visions such as the one seen by some people in Fatima, Portugal in 1917 of visual phenomena associated with the Sun? One might argue that the conditions here were unreliable, as many did not see the visual phenomena, and there are notable psychological effects that can take place when in a crowd which would call into question the validity of something experienced.

It seems very difficult, on examination, to be able to claim, as Swinburne does, that most religious experiences don't take place under unreliable conditions. For instance, one could point to almost countless environmental inputs that might influence the nature of a religious experience and make it unreliable. They could be physiological - fasting and other religious practices; psychological - the effect of environment, lighting, on emotions; or sociological, within crowds - as part of the expected belief system within which one was brought up. Surely these are all factors which must have an impact on any argument using the Principle of Credulity?

Swinburne's second and third kind of evidence both reduce to the question of whether it is reasonable to believe in God. They are answered by Swinburne in his cumulative case argument. So it is worth spending some time examining this.

SWINBURNE'S CUMULATIVE CASE ARGUMENT

Swinburne puts forward a cumulative case for belief in God. He examines the traditional arguments for God and concludes that together they inductively raise the probability of theism. It is worth going into his argument a little, but don't be put off by the technical-sounding terminology - it is quite straightforward:

> Let us call an argument in which the premisses make the conclusion probable [i.e. more likely than not to be true] a correct P-inductive argument. Let us call an argument in which the premisses add to the probability of the conclusion (i.e., make the conclusion more likely or more probable than it would otherwise be) a correct C-inductive argument. In this case let us say that the premisses "confirm" the conclusion. Among correct C-inductive arguments some will obviously be stronger than others, in the sense that in some the premisses will raise the probability of the conclusion more than the premisses do in other arguments.

Swinburne is here assessing the intrinsic probability of theism. He maintains that the traditional arguments for God such as the teleological, cosmological and so on, are **C-INDUCTIVE ARGUMENTS**, in other words, they add to the probability of the universe having a theistic explanation. Also important to note, is that the arguments taken together are not seen as a single thread by Swinburne, but rather interface with each other, such that while none are particularly strong alone, together they have a persuasive value. The sum is greater than the parts. A useful way of looking at this is to consider the usual objection to the cumulative case argument - one leaky bucket doesn't hold water - and ten leaky buckets all stacked together don't either. So ten ineffective arguments when combined cannot make one good argument. What is often not appreciated, however, is that this is true if you are trying to prove a conclusion, but not necessarily so in the sort of probabilistic use that Swinburne puts the arguments to. The arguments are here presented as merely adding to the probability of the theistic hypothesis.

So in fact, ten leaky buckets, when stacked together so that none of the holes overlap, will hold water quite successfully! This can be seen when we consider that not all of the arguments fail at precisely the same points, so that one argument may actually reinforce another one at its weakest point. For instance, the cosmological argument is often seen to be weak in that it doesn't point to anything more than some kind of cause - so only gets to deism. However, some moral arguments will point to the existence of a loving creator, and thus cancel out some of the force of this weakness.

All in all, Swinburne's argument is recognised for the way in which it put a new emphasis on the arguments in natural theology whilst attempting to sidestep some of the challenges from evidentialism. Some might consider, however, that the principles of credulity and testimony cannot bear the weight that he puts on them. We have seen above the problems with these principles.

As a final point worth noting, the words of CS Lewis on miracles apply fruitfully to an evaluation of Swinburne's principles:

> In all my life I have only met one person who claims to have seen a ghost. And the interesting thing about the story is that that person disbelieved in the immortal soul before she saw the ghost and still disbelieves after seeing it. She says that what she saw must have been an illusion or trick of the mind. And obviously she may be right. Seeing is not believing. For this reason, the

question whether miracles occur can never be answered simply by experience. Every event which might claim to be a miracle is, in the last resort, something presented to our senses, something seen, heard, touched, smelled, or tasted. And the senses are not infallible. If anything extraordinary seems to have happened, we can always say that we have been the victims of an illusion. If we hold a philosophy which excludes the supernatural, this always shall be what we say. What we learn from experience depends on the kind of philosophy we bring to experience. It is therefore useless to appeal to experience before we have settled, as well as we can, the philosophical question.

And this is precisely Swinburne's method. He realises that the principles of credulity and testimony will only work if prior to them we have settled the philosophical question of the existence of God. This is why an evaluation of his cumulative case argument is needed before you can evaluate the effectiveness of the principles. Ultimately, any attempt to prove God purely from religious experience is unlikely to be convincing, but Swinburne has at least shown that it is not coherent or consistent to dismiss testimonies of religious experiences simply because they are religious experiences, an important step in the debate about religious experience.

SELF-ASSESSMENT QUESTIONS

1. What "principle of rationality" does the Principle of Credulity rely on?

2. Why is the Principle of Credulity axiomatic?

3. What are the similarities and differences between Swinburne's argument and those discussed in chapter 5?

4. Name the other principles of Swinburne's argument and explain how they support it.

5. Write a list of strengths and weaknesses of the Principle of Credulity.

6. Explain how the Principle of Credulity and Ockham's Razor work together in Swinburne's argument.

7. How does Swinburne answer the objections to the Principle of Credulity?

8. What are the three types of evidence which would count against the validity of religious experience according to Swinburne?

9. How does the cumulative case argument support the Principle of Credulity?

10. Do you agree with the "ten leaky buckets" analogy? Why or why not?

FURTHER READING

FRANKS DAVIS, C - The Evidential Force of Religious Experience, OUP, 1989

SWINBURNE, R - Is There a God?, OUP, 2005

Religious experience and the question of epistemology

KEY WORDS

- **DISANALOGIES** - Differences between two things.

- **DOXASTIC PRACTICES** - William Alston's term for belief-forming practices within a religion.

- **EVIDENTIALISM** - The theory that knowledge can be built on a foundation of evidence from sense data.

- **FOUNDATIONALISM** - Epistemological theory which holds that knowledge can be built on some self-evident foundation (such as sense-data), without need for further justification, thus stopping infinite regress of explanations.

- **PARADIGMATIC** - Held as the paradigm for a situation, an exemplar, or framework within which theories work.

- **PERCEPT** - That which is perceived.

- **PROPERLY BASIC** - Describing a belief which is held by a person as self-evident or evident to the senses.

- **QUESTION-BEGGING** - Describing a fallacious argument that assumes the situation it is intending to prove.

- **SELF-AUTHENTICATING** - An experience in which the perception entails the existence of the percept.

- **VICIOUS CIRCLE CHALLENGE** - Challenge relating to religious experience in which the experience is formed by the prior beliefs of the person, and vice versa.

We finished the last chapter with the claim that any attempt to prove God purely from religious experience is unlikely to be convincing. However, some have claimed that it is possible to do such a thing. They claim that a purported experience of God is itself enough to justify believing in God on the basis of it. Experiences such as these are often called **SELF-AUTHENTICATING**. The idea that an experience entails the existence of its **PERCEPT** has been heavily criticised by **ANTONY FLEW** among others, and is hard to maintain in the face of objections based on such phenomena as hallucinations, mirages, delusions and so on. As we have seen, its attraction lies in the fact that it seems to root perception of God in some more basic, fundamental type of vision which seems to perceive reality "as it is", unmediated by discursive thought. We find this idea as a strong thread going back to the Romantics:

> If the doors of perception were cleansed every thing would appear to man as it is, Infinite. For man has closed himself up, till he sees all things thro' narrow chinks of his cavern. (William Blake, The Marriage of Heaven and Hell)

However, such an idea, as I mentioned previously, actually has its roots in a Platonic view of reality; Blake is alluding to Plato's Cave in his poem - in which the inherent unreliability of our sense perception, the shadows on the cave wall - is transcended by an interior struggle to perceive truth. Whilst this has in modern epistemology been flattened into a priori reasoning, it was in truth originally a mystical ascent, and can be seen as such in the writings of Pseudo-Dionysius, Plotinus, Augustine, Meister Eckhart, St John of the Cross and many others.

So on the one hand the modern notion of a "self-authenticating" experience can be seen as an attempt to transcend the Kantian division into noumenal and phenomenal which doesn't work, but on the other hand there is an important sense in which that division itself misrepresents the Platonic inheritance which distinguished between ratio and intellectus (see chapter 3). In this chapter we will look at attempts to move beyond this dilemma.

Self-authentication has been an important part of some more modern accounts of religious experience:

> The popularisation of the discourse about religious experience more or less coincides with the turn to subjectivity in modernity. William James' Varieties of Religious Experience greatly helps the entrenchment of the idea of "religious experience". Rudolf Otto does a similar job for the idea of "numinous experience". These authors are all concerned to show that the capacity for religious experience is somehow natural to the human psyche. Their work can be seen as efforts to break away from the modern epistemological straitjacket of British empiricism or Kantian agnosticism.

> However, they are not always clear whether religious experience is merely a feeling or a cognitive experience. So these thinkers do not explicitly formulate any argument from religious experience, that is, the argument that the occurrence of religious experience provides grounds or justification for the existence of God. However, the argument from religious experience is now defended by sophisticated philosophers.

(Kai-Man Kwan, Can Religious Experience Provide Justification for the Belief in God?)

We saw in Chapter 2 how the attempt to break out of the Kantian epistemological straitjacket led to the partially "self-authenticating" positions of James and Otto. It is important to realise that these studies are not straightforward articulations of philosophical arguments based on religious experiences, even though there are certainly a lot of philosophical issues raised by them. In this chapter I want to look at how "sophisticated philosophers" have moved beyond self-authentication in the search for valid arguments for religious experience.

She is right to claim this, and indeed this kind of argument is helpful in countering over-simplistic sceptical challenges because it shows that the epistemological issues in religious experience are not unique to the religious case.

Arguments from the analogy with sense-perception

William Wainwright argues for the cognitive value of religious experience thus:

- Sense-perception is paradigmatic of a cognitive type of experience.

- If the analogy is close between a mystical experience and a sense experience then the mystical experience is cognitive.

- Both types of experience are noetic (have an intentional object, involve belief that that object really exists, give rise to checkable claims about states of affairs, and in both cases there are checking procedures to determine if the object is real and whether the experience is a genuine perception of it).

- Therefore the analogy is close enough to warrant mystical experience probably being cognitive.

- If it could be shown that we had independent reasons to believe mystics, we could say mystical experience was actually cognitive.

- We do have such reasons - natural theology and the sanity and sanctity of mystics provide those reasons.

- Therefore mystical experience is actually cognitive.

Even if we are sceptical of Wainwright's independent reasons to believe mystics' claims we still have an argument which claims mystical experience is probably cognitive, based on the analogies with sense-perception outweighing the disanalogies. But do they?

Franks Davis claims that the most problematic area here is the "checking procedures" part of the argument. The checking procedures we have in the case of sense-perception include:

- using technology like cameras, video footage and so on

- having independent verification from others

- the perceiver being of sound mind and body

- corroboration from other senses

- consistency with background knowledge

- the perceived object remains the same under closer observation.

An examination of possible equivalent checking procedures in the domain of religious experience shows us such tests as:

- internal and external consistency (they must not conflict with each other)

- moral and spiritual fruits (James emphasises these)

- consistency with orthodox doctrine

- evaluation of the psychological condition of the subject.

There is clearly some overlap - for instance, the subject's mental condition in both cases is important, and in the consistency criteria, but the sceptic's challenge here is that:

- even if the religious experience satisfies these criteria for the most part, they are still presupposing the validity of the religious doctrine, and

- they omit the strongest types of test for sense-perception - that of corroboration by other people and technology, and the ability to predict successfully.

The first point is related to the **VICIOUS CIRCLE CHALLENGE**, which argues that because perception involves interpretation, people see what their prior assumptions lead them to see; rather than religious experiences being a basis for faith, they are generated by faith.

With this point, is it the case that the checking procedures are viciously circular? Perhaps consistency with doctrine could be cited, but the other tests are not necessarily so.

Franks Davis has this to say about the technological checks demanded by the second point:

> *Even judgements about sense perception are not immune from the influence of prevailing dogma - the test of consistency with background knowledge ensures that. We may laugh now at those churchmen who refused to look through Galileo's telescope, but they believed that experience mediated by a manmade instrument could never be as sure as metaphysical doctrines, in this case the doctrine of the perfection of heavenly bodies. Nowadays, in contrast, we place so much faith in*

technology that it is sometimes made the ultimate arbiter in matters of sense perception - "The camera doesn't lie!"

But it is also the case that such tests are not appropriate to religious experience, particularly the ability to predict successfully - therefore, the analogy between religious experience and sense experience is not very close, and Wainwright's argument fails.

But there is also a more serious criticism of these types of argument from the analogy with sense perception:

"The criteria of veridicality for sense perception cannot themselves be inductively justified, for one must appeal in the inductive process to the very sorts of experience one is trying to show to be veridical." (Caroline Franks Davis)

So arguments from religious experience based on the analogy with sense experience are misguided, in that sense experience itself cannot be saved from the sceptic's doubt by appeal to other sense experience, as this is **QUESTION-BEGGING** and circular.

This is the issue with evidential **FOUNDATIONALISM**. Evidential foundationalists believe that our knowledge has to be built on the foundation of sense experiences because only they are the indubitable "given", free from interpretations, and are open to public confirmation.

Evidential foundationalism, for the reasons described above, has shown itself to be inherently flawed. We have already seen in chapter 4 that an argument which credits religious experience with prima facie evidential force can be formulated without the need to rely on analogies from sense-perception. Such analogies are susceptible to the shortcomings of the epistemological position of evidential foundationalism.

"Personal Encounter" arguments

> There cannot be a living awareness of God as personal unless we realise that God meets our wills with his value-resistances always in the plane of our personal relations with one another. Unless a man is meeting God with the utmost seriousness in that plane, unless he is realising that the one supreme achievement in life from God's point of view is to be in right relations to the men and women who cross his path, and this at any cost of resistance to his own natural feelings and impulses, he cannot meet him to much profit in any other plane of life, nor certainly, grow into a living sense of him as personal. *(HH Farmer)*

The argument that religious experience is a personal encounter has been formulated most famously by Martin Buber in I And Thou, in which he describes God as the "Thou that by its nature cannot become It". There are certainly many persuasive points to this formulation of the argument.

- Our most important relationships with our friends and those we love have an immediacy that seems appropriate to the relationship with God.

- Such encounters go beyond mere inferred knowledge of the existence of another - they are intuitive.

- Knowledge by acquaintance is often seen as a deeper and more direct sense of the word knowledge - as in "I know John".

It preserves a large part of the biblical sense of God as more than a mere object, and is the preferred metaphor used in the writings of mystics from many different traditions - see for instance the metaphor of the lover and the beloved in such diverse places as the Song of Songs, the Sufi mystic Jelalludin Rumi, St John of the Cross and many others.

We feel we know intuitively that the people we meet and have relationships with are conscious beings with interior lives of their own, but we do not infer that knowledge from experience.

▸ **Problems with trying to base an argument on the "personal encounter" analogy**

Knowledge of friends and people around us is completely uncontroversial, whereas knowledge of God isn't, therefore arguments which go beyond a simple sense of a personal encounter are relevant.

Even though there can be "factual" statements about our friends and about God (eg loving, powerful, etc), we can be mistaken about the sense of encounter we have with them.

The argument rests on the fact that personal encounters are taken as prima facie veridical (ie veridical unless good reasons can be given for rejecting them), but in the case of encounters with God, one of the things at issue is whether they are veridical or not! Therefore it is a question-begging argument.

Experiencing-as

Belief in God, under this argument, is a matter of seeing in a different light the very same facts which an atheist sees. The well-known paper "Gods" by John Wisdom expresses this in the parable of the "Invisible Gardener", which many students will recognise from Flew's use of it in "Theology and Falsification".

In that parable different patterns are discerned in the same set of data which lead two people to different conclusions about it, eg one explorer seizes on the lack of a gardener and rambling plants to argue that a clearing in the woods is wild, while the other finds signs of cultivation which leads him to believe there is a gardener.

John Hick used "experiencing-as" as an explanation for religious experience. He bases his account on the well-known "duck-rabbit" figure used by Wittgenstein to explain his theory of linguistic meaning - that words get their meaning from context - and equally we can experience the drawing on the page as a duck or a rabbit, depending on the way we look at it. In the same way, Hick argues:

> ... there is a sense in which the religious man and the atheist both live in the same world, and another sense in which they live consciously in different worlds ... [the world] has for each a different meaning and significance; for one does and the other does not experience life as a continual interaction with the transcendent God.

Hick argues that all experience is "experiencing-as" - thus the world for some will be experienced religiously. While seeming to account for certain types of indirect religious experience, this theory has some serious flaws:

- It is not clear that there is some set of raw data, neutral experience or bare facts upon which we impose our different interpretations - facts are only neutral in relation to a set of mutually agreed theories, so will always involve a certain amount of interpretation. Franks Davis says: "In Wisdom's gardener parable it is assumed that both men have the same idea about what counts as a weed, what as a garden plant, what indeed as a garden, and this is what makes it seem so obvious that they are in agreement about all the facts."

- Most religious experience is private, theory-laden and culturally overlaid, therefore doesn't count as the kind of neutral middle ground about which a theist and an atheist can differ in interpretation.

- It doesn't account for direct experiences such as theistic mystical encounters.

- "Experiencing-as" only really works for certain types of permanently ambiguous forms of experience, about which there is no privileged authoritative explanation, not all experience is of this kind.

Basic belief

Alvin Plantinga maintains that the evidentialist objection ("It is wrong always and everywhere to believe something on insufficient evidence." - W K Clifford) rests on what he calls classical foundationalism.

Classical foundationalism says that a belief must be either inferred from other rational beliefs, be self-evident (2+2=4), incorrigible (beyond correction, eg my hand hurts), or evident to the senses (I can see a cat). Classical foundationalists call these last three "properly basic" beliefs, beliefs which are prima facie justified.

Plantinga rejects this entire scheme and puts in its place what he calls "reformed epistemology", which is really a more lenient version of foundationalism, in which belief in God can, under certain conditions, be what he calls "properly basic".

He is able to do this by showing that classical foundationalism is self-referentially inconsistent (see below).

▸ **Strengths**

- Plantinga "shows that classical foundationalism is self-referentially inconsistent: it is itself neither inferred from rational beliefs, self-evident, incorrigible, or evident to the senses, hence by its own criteria it is not a rational belief". (Franks Davis)

- In reformulating the criteria for proper basicality, Plantinga can allow beliefs which had to be rejected in classical foundationalism, even though to do so would be absurd - beliefs about the existence of other persons and memories.

- Plantinga articulates "dispositions to believe" certain things, which entail belief in God. These are such things as a spontaneous feeling of gratitude at the sweetness of life, feelings of guilt when one has acted poorly, a need to cry out and ask for God's protection when one is in danger and so on. These in his reformed epistemology would rank alongside the disposition to believe what your senses tell you.

- These dispositions to believe would counter the "flying teapot" objection (as formulated by Bertrand Russell - if I am to believe that there is an invisible intangible God, aren't I equally compelled to believe that an invisible intangible teapot orbits the Earth?).

▸ Weaknesses

- Some dispositions to believe are unreliable, eg the disposition to think the worst of a person you don't like.

- Any account resting on such dispositions to believe is far too simplistic. Children generally have dispositions to believe in the tooth fairy, etc. This plays into the hands of people like Dawkins.

- Not actually an attempt to persuade the atheist that God exists - just to show that belief in God might not be irrational even if no justification can be given for that belief.

CONCLUSION

Ultimately, the different types of argument we have reviewed in this chapter can be seen to each have their own particular attraction, even if none of them seems particularly compelling in the final breakdown. However, there is one other type of argument from religious experience - the cumulative case argument, which we have already examined in greater length in Chapter 4. To many philosophers this type of sophisticated argument for religious experience is the strongest formulated so far.

This is because in formulating a principle of rationality so basic that even religious experiences are subsumed under it, Swinburne does not have to rely on weak analogies or dubious "dispositions to believe".

Hopefully in this chapter you have been able to see some of the context and background behind Swinburne's argument, which should ideally make it easier to understand and evaluate.

SELF-ASSESSMENT QUESTIONS

1. Explain the challenges to a "self-authenticating" account of religious experience.

2. What is the evidentialist challenge? In what ways have philosophers developed responses to it?

3. Explain an argument against religious experience using the disanalogies with sense-perception.

4. Why might such an argument be flawed?

5. Explain William Wainwright's argument from analogy with sense-perception.

6. Explain how the flaws inherent in evidential foundationalism limit the effectiveness of Wainwright's argument.

7. How might you formulate an argument for God based on "personal encounter"?

8. What are the strengths and weaknesses of such an argument?

9. Why does the "experiencing-as" argument for religious experience misrepresent the nature of experience?

10. Give a brief description of Plantinga's argument from basic belief and explain its strengths and weaknesses.

FURTHER READING

FRANKS DAVIS, C - The Evidential Force of Religious Experience, OUP, 1989

ROWE & WAINWRIGHT - Philosophy of Religion, Selected Readings, 3rd ed., Harcourt Brace, 1998 (Chapter 5)

HICK, J - Classical and Contemporary Readings in the Philosophy of Religion, 3rd ed. Prentice Hall, 1990

Postscript

Matthew Livermore teaches Religious Studies to A level at Coloma Convent Girls' School in Croydon. He has also taught Theory of Knowledge for IB and is a trained teacher of Philosophy for Children (P4C).

He runs a philosophy club, and is interested in helping students to develop the thinking skills at the heart of the curriculum, which he sees as increasingly important in a rapidly changing educational environment. He runs a blog on Philosophy of Religion - mrlivermore.wordpress.com - and can be found on Twitter: @mrlivermore.

He is also a keen artist, and sees the practice of art as a type of philosophical activity, wherein the artist is engaged in a search for truth and veracity, in a dialogue between self and world which constantly challenges his own assumptions about the nature of what is seen and experienced.

Lightning Source UK Ltd.
Milton Keynes UK
UKOW04f1302131014

240024UK00002B/100/P